Alfred Bishop Mason, John Joseph Lalor

The Primer of political Economy

In sixteen Definitions and forty Propositions

Alfred Bishop Mason, John Joseph Lalor

The Primer of political Economy
In sixteen Definitions and forty Propositions

ISBN/EAN: 9783337079581

Printed in Europe, USA, Canada, Australia, Japan

Cover: Foto ©ninafisch / pixelio.de

More available books at **www.hansebooks.com**

THE PRIMER

OF

POLITICAL ECONOMY;

IN SIXTEEN DEFINITIONS AND FORTY PROPOSITIONS.

BY

ALPRED B. MASON AND JOHN J. LALOR.

CHICAGO:
JANSEN, McCLURG & COMPANY.
1875.

PRESS OF
KNIGHT & LEONARD.
CHICAGO

PREFACE.

This little book makes no claim beyond that expressed in its title. It is simply a Primer. We have written it in the hope that it may be used as a text-book in the common schools of the country. The time that can be allotted to the study of political economy in these schools does not exceed a term or two; and the ordinary text-books are far too large to be even superficially mastered within that time. The Primer, on the contrary, can be thoroughly learned without any undue interference with the other studies of the course. The experience of one of the authors in teaching political economy, for several years, to boys and girls has convinced us that the arrangement by definitions and propositions which we have adopted is the best for the purpose here indicated. Especial prominence has been given to the more practical applications of the science. The pages devoted to coöperation are the result of personal study of the subject in England and Germany. While the Primer is designed for use as a text-book, we trust that persons out of school may read it with some pleasure and profit.

The standard English, French, German and American works on political economy have been freely consulted in the preparation of the book. We have aimed to give, in simple words and with copious illustration, the well-settled doctrines of the fascinating science. The distinction between the real and the possible wage-fund has not, we believe, been stated before. It may serve to reconcile opposing theories on the wage-fund question. With this exception, the Primer contains only old truths in new forms. A few pages in it are transcripts, more or less exact, from articles written by the authors for the Chicago *Tribune*.

The experience in teaching political economy already referred to is our excuse for a word of suggestion. The scholar should be required to give the definitions and the captions of the propositions *verbatim*, but mere memorizing should not be carried beyond this. It is far better that the explanation of the one and the proof of the other should be in the pupil's own words. One of the best tests of knowledge is to ask for original illustrations.

ALFRED B. MASON.

JOHN J. LALOR.

CHICAGO, June, 1875.

TABLE OF CONTENTS.

THE PRIMER OF POLITICAL ECONOMY.

DEFINITION 1. *Political Economy is the science which teaches the laws that regulate the production, distribution and exchange of wealth.*

Everything in this world is governed by law. Human laws are those made by men. All others are natural laws. A law providing for the education of children in schools is a human law. The law that children shall keep growing, if they live, until they are men or women, and shall then slowly decay and at last die, is a natural law. An apple falls from a tree and the earth moves around the sun in obedience to natural laws. The laws which regulate the production, distribution and exchange of wealth are of both kinds. The more important ones, however, are natural.

DEFINITION 2. *Wealth is anything for which something can be got in exchange.*

Many useful things are not wealth. Air is one of the most useful things in the world. A person deprived of it would die. Water is a very useful thing, too. But air and water are not wealth, because they can be got without giving anything in exchange for them. Sometimes, however, each of them may be wealth. If a man had to live in a diving-bell, he would have to pay in some way for the air sent down in pipes for him to breathe. In a desert, a little bottle of water will sell for a good deal. Men sometimes pay for the right to use the water of a stream to turn a mill-wheel. In these cases, the air and the water are wealth, because something can be got in exchange for them.

In order to tell whether or not any particular thing is wealth, we must ask, "Can something be got in exchange for it?" If something can, then it is wealth.

A coat is wealth. So are houses, corn, diamonds, a doctor's skill, money, shovels, the ability to make furniture, furniture itself, bricks and thousands of other things.

(9)

DEFINITION 3. *A commodity is wealth in tangible form.*

The list just given of things that are wealth contains some things that are commodities and some that are not.

A coat, a house, corn, a diamond, money, a shovel, furniture and a brick are commodities, because they are wealth in a form which can be touched.

A doctor's skill and the ability to make furniture cannot be touched. Therefore they are not commodities, although they are wealth.

DEFINITION 4. *Capital is wealth saved, and used in production.*

It is important to remember that capital is wealth that is (1) saved, and (2) used in production. Land is wealth, but it is not capital, because, although it is used to produce crops, nobody has saved it. So $10,000 in money locked up in a safe is wealth, but it is not capital, because, although somebody has saved it, it is not used to produce more wealth.

Food eaten by men who work is capital. Money used to pay the wages of workmen is capital. Tools are capital.

Land is a natural agent, like water, air, the force of gravitation, etc. It is the most important of all the natural agents.

PROPOSITION I.

To produce wealth, three things are required,— natural agents, capital, and labor.

The production of vegetable food needs, first, a natural agent in the shape of the land on which the food grows; second, the labor of clearing, fencing, plowing, digging and planting the land and of gathering the crops, and perhaps, as in the case of wheat, the labor of grinding the grain into flour and of cooking it afterwards; and, third, capital in the shape of the tools used in all these occupations, the seed employed in planting, the clothing and the food consumed by the laborers, etc.

In the production of a doctor's skill, the principal natural agent is again the land. This has produced

most of the food which the body must consume in order
to exist while the mind gains the required skill. The
capital is the food and clothing consumed by the doctor
while studying, the cost of providing him with shelter,
and the money paid for his tuition. The labor is that
spent in teaching him and in caring for him from the day
of his birth.

In the production of linen, the natural agents directly
at·work are the land on which the manufactory stands
and on which the raw material (flax) grew and the power
which makes the machinery go. This power may be the
air, turning a windmill; or heat, acting on water in a
boiler and so creating steam; or water, turning a water-
wheel. The labor is that spent in raising the flax and
that of the men, women and children who spin thread
from the flax and weave the thread into linen cloth, and
also that of the persons who built the manufactory and
invented and made the machinery, and, again, that of the
persons who now manage the works. The capital consists of the building, the machinery, the money used in
paying wages, the flax consumed, etc.

Thus, in these three very different cases, the production of wealth requires natural agents, capital, and labor.
No case of production can be imagined in which these
three forces do not combine. But a law to which no
exception can be found may be taken as true.

Therefore, to produce wealth, three things are required,— natural agents, capital, and labor.

PROPOSITION II.

**Natural agents which are limited in quantity, are wealth; and
those which are practically unlimited, are not wealth.**

If anything is unlimited in quantity, anyone who
wishes it can get it. Air is an example. Everybody
can get it free, and therefore nobody will give anything
in exchange for it. But if a person could get control of
all the air and take it away from everybody else, he

could get a great deal in exchange for it, because people would have to have it or die. Therefore, if air were limited in quantity, it would be wealth.

In thickly-settled countries, land is strictly limited in quantity; none of it is left unowned, and therefore none of it can be got free. Every acre of it is wealth. Something can be got in exchange for it. In unsettled countries, however, land is practically unlimited in quantity. That is, there is more of it there than anybody wants. A man who owned one of a hundred similar islands near the North Pole could not exchange it for anything, because anyone who wished an island in that neighborhood could get another as good as this for nothing.

Water is usually practically unlimited in quantity. Two cases have been mentioned (see explanation of Def. 2) in which water is limited in quantity. In both these cases, something can be got in exchange for it. Therefore, when limited, it is wealth.

We see, then, that the same natural agent is some·times wealth and sometimes not wealth, according as it is limited or unlimited in quantity.

Therefore, natural agents which are limited in quantity are wealth, and those which are practically unlimited are not wealth.

DEFINITION 5. *Capital is divided into fixed and circulating.*

Capital is used in two ways. It is *fixed* in buildings, machinery, tools, the permanent improvements of land (such as drainage), canals, railroads, etc. It *circulates* when used in paying wages, buying raw material (like flax for the manufacture of linen), etc.

Fixed capital lasts a long time. The things produced by its aid use up only a small part of it, year after year. If a manufacturer of linen has a building, machinery, etc., this fixed capital can be employed in the manufacture of very many thousand yards of linen before it is worn out. Still, the production of each yard wears out the works a very little.

Circulating capital is all used up by being used once. When the manufacturer produces a yard of linen, he has entirely parted with the flax in it and with the labor spent upon the flax. When he sells the piece of cloth, he must get enough for it to replace all he has spent for these two things and to pay for the part of his fixed capital which has been used up in the manufacture, and, if possible, to yield him a profit.

Thus the product must repay *all* the circulating capital and *part* of the fixed capital used in its production.

A crop of corn, in order to give the farmer a profit, must sell for more than the cost of the seed sown and the labor spent in preparing the ground and in sowing and gathering the grain, *plus* an amount equal to the harm done to the fencing, drainage, etc.

PROPOSITION III.

The proportion of fixed to circulating capital depends upon the way in which capital is used.

If a shirt-manufacturer hires a number of women to sew for him at their homes, his capital is almost entirely circulating. He uses nearly all of it in buying cloth, thread, buttons, etc., and in paying wages. If he builds a large manufactory and stocks it with machinery and has his employés work there, a much larger part of his capital becomes fixed.

A very large proportion of the capital of a railway company is fixed in the shape of roadbed, rails, cars, locomotives, car-shops and stations. A very small part of the capital of a dealer in coal is fixed. He needs only a yard in which to store his stock, a few teams and a small office. His main use for his capital is in buying coal at the mines, defraying the cost of its transportation and paying the wages of his employés.

A similar analysis of any other business would show that the capital used in it was divided into fixed and circulating, according to the nature of the particular industry.

Therefore, the proportion of fixed to circulating capital depends upon the way in which capital is used.

PROPOSITION IV.

The stock of capital is kept up by constant reproduction.

The definition of capital (Def. 4) shows that it must be used in order to be capital. Using it destroys it. This is true of both circulating and fixed capital.

When a yard of linen is manufactured, the flax in it, as flax, no longer exists. The food consumed by the workmen who made it no longer exists. The flax and the food are circulating capital. Using them has destroyed them.

A building, which is fixed capital, is not used up by being used once, but it is gradually worn out by use. It has to be repaired constantly. If the repairs are neglected, it finally tumbles down.

The only difference, in this respect, between fixed and circulating capital is, that the first is destroyed bit by bit whenever it is used, while the second is entirely destroyed whenever it is used. A spade, which is fixed capital, may be used to dig a great many potatoes out of the ground, but part of it is worn away each time. A potato, which is circulating capital, can be used only once, and then it is wholly consumed.

Now if the yard of linen is not worth more than all the capital destroyed in making it, the world's stock of capital is less than it would have been had the linen not been made. But if the linen is worth more than all the capital destroyed in making it, then the capital has been more than reproduced, and the world's stock of it has been increased.

As capital must (Def. 4) be used in production, and as using it always destroys it, it is evident that the only way to keep up the stock of capital is to use it so that it will produce, by the time it is destroyed, at least an equal amount of capital.

Therefore, the stock of capital is kept up by constant reproduction.

PROPOSITION V.

The amount of capital used, measures the amount of labor employed.

To produce wealth (Prop. I), both capital and labor are required. Therefore, in order that labor may be employed, capital must be. The more capital, the more labor. For capital cannot produce wealth, unless labor works with it.

The reason why capital measures labor, instead of labor's measuring capital, is, that the capitalist takes the first step in production by providing buildings, machinery, tools, and usually raw materials. Then, but not till then, labor takes up the task. Capital must act first, and labor second. Until capital acts, labor cannot. Therefore, labor has to wait for capital to begin, and is dependent upon capital for employment.

Labor also depends upon capital for support while being employed. The capitalist advances to the laborer, in the shape of wages, the food, clothing, shelter, etc., needed by the latter, and finally repays himself for the advance out of the proceeds of the wealth the laborer has helped to produce. A manufacturer of jewelry, for instance, first uses his capital in providing a suitable work-room and the necessary tools. Then he buys the needed gold, and the other raw materials. Then he hires labor. The amount of labor he engages must depend upon the size of his work-room, the number of his tools, and the quantity of gold, etc., which he has to be made into ornaments. These things all depend upon the amount of capital he has invested. Moreover, before he can sell anything, it must be manufactured. While it is being manufactured he must pay out money to his workmen without getting any money from his customers. In order to do this, he must have capital.

Therefore, since labor is employed by capital, and supported by capital, the amount of capital used measures the amount of labor employed.

DEFINITION 6. *Demand for a thing consists of a desire to buy it, on the part of persons who have something to give in exchange for it.*

DEFINITION 7. *Supply of a thing consists of a desire to sell it, on the part of persons who possess it.*

Thus a demand for cotton consists of the desire to buy cotton in the minds of persons who have money or something else to give in exchange for the cotton. If they have no money and no purchasing power in any other form, however much they may want cotton, there is no demand for it in the politico-economical meaning of the word.

So a supply of cotton consists of a desire to sell cotton, in the minds of persons who have cotton to give in exchange for money or any other commodity.

PROPOSITION VI.

Supply in excess of demand causes prices to fall, and demand in excess of supply causes prices to rise.

When the supply of anything exceeds the demand for it, each person who wishes to sell the particular thing will be afraid that his stock of it will be the portion of the supply which the demand will not reach. He will, therefore, put down his prices in order to induce buyers to take his wares instead of those of his neighbor. Each seller will do this, consequently general prices will fall. If there is a demand for nine brooms, and a supply of ten, each broom-seller will fear that one of his brooms will be left on his hands. To prevent this, he will mark down his prices; therefore, brooms will be cheaper. Hence, greater production and greater cheapness go hand in hand.

When demand for anything exceeds supply of it, each person who wishes to buy the particular thing will be afraid that the whole supply of it will be absorbed by other buyers, and that he will not be able to get what he wants. He will therefore offer more in exchange for it, in order to induce the owner to sell to him instead of to his neighbor. Each buyer will do this; consequently, general prices will rise. If five persons want horses, and there are only four horses for sale, each of the five will be willing to pay something extra rather than not have any horse at all. The four highest bidders will get the four horses; therefore, horses will be dearer. Hence, scanty production means dear goods.

This demonstration proves the "first law of demand and supply,"— namely, supply in excess of demand causes prices to fall, and demand in excess of supply causes prices to rise.

PROPOSITION VII. ·

A demand for a thing tends to produce a supply of that thing at a fair price.

If there is a demand for anything, it will pay capitalists to use their capital in supplying that thing; they will therefore do so. If the profits they make are very large, other capitalists will be tempted to go into the business. Then competition between the manufacturers (Prop. VI) will cut down the price of the article. It will not, however, cut it down, except temporarily, below a fair price, that is, a price which will pay for the natural agents, capital and labor expended upon its production. For if the price falls below this limit, capital will be withdrawn from the industry. This will diminish the production. The resulting scarcity of the thing (Prop. VI) will raise its price again.

In 1869 there was a sort of mania for velocipedes. Many boys and some men wanted them. This created a demand for velocipedes. The demand was at first in excess of the supply; prices were therefore high. A great supply of velocipedes followed; then their prices fell. Pretty soon it was discovered that there was not much amusement after all in riding on a velocipede. The demand for them became almost nothing; their man-

2

ufacture stopped almost entirely. But there was a great
stock of them on hand; they were therefore sold for very
small prices. Now there is a little demand for velocipedes
for children, and these can be bought at a fair price.

In the case of things,— such as the paintings of a dead
artist,— which are strictly limited in quantity, demand
cannot produce a supply at a fair price, because the necessary supply cannot be produced, no matter how much
capital and labor are spent in the effort. But in the case of
all things which can be produced in any quantity — that is,
in the case of nearly everything — this proposition applies.

Hence, we have the "second law of supply and demand,"— namely, a demand for a thing tends to produce
a supply of that thing at a fair price.

DEFINITION 8. *Consumption is productive or unpro-ductive.*

Consumption which increases the productive powers of the
community is productive. Needed food eaten by a man who
works is productively consumed. The iron which is melted and
then made into a rail which is afterwards used, is productively
consumed. So are the tiles used in draining a farm.

Consumption which does not increase the productive powers
of the community is unproductive. The food and clothing of an
idler are unproductively consumed. If a workingman, who
needs only a pound of food a day, eats a pound and a half, the
extra half-pound is unproductively consumed. Iron melted and
flung away is unproductively consumed. Silks, velvets and
laces are usually unproductively consumed. So is tobacco.

PROPOSITION VIII.

Productive consumption benefits labor.

Productive consumption (see explanation of Def. 8)
increases the productive powers of the community. Increasing the productive powers of a community increases
its stock of wealth. The larger this is, the greater is apt
to be the capital of the community. And if more capital is used, more labor (Prop. V) is employed. Hence

productive consumption causes a greater employment of labor.

Therefore productive consumption benefits labor.

PROPOSITION IX.

Unproductive consumption hurts labor.

When anything is consumed without increasing the productive powers of a community, that community's stock of wealth is decreased by just the value of the thing thus consumed. If one thousand people each eat one-fourth of a pound more food per day than they need, the community's stock of wealth suffers a needless loss of two hundred and fifty pounds of food a day.

Unproductive consumption decreases a community's stock of wealth. If a country's wealth is lessened, the country's capital is apt to be less. But the less capital (Prop. V), the less labor.

Suppose a man pays $250 a year for food, one-fifth of which he does not need, and therefore consumes unproductively. If he stops this unproductive consumption, the capital and labor employed in producing the $50 worth of food now wasted will be used in producing something else for which there is a demand, say shoes. The man will have the $50 he saves every year to use in producing a third thing, say books. Then the community will still have all the food it needs, and will have besides, as the result of this stoppage of unproductive consumption, more shoes and more books, of neither of which did it have enough before.

In this case, the price of food remains the same, because the demand has diminished with the supply. The prices of both shoes and books are lower, because (Prop. VI) the supply has increased.

There *was* only one fund used in production, that is, in hiring labor. This was the fund used to produce the extra food. This fund still exists, and is used to produce shoes. But now there is another fund, which is used to produce books. There are, therefore, since the unproductive consumption ceased, two funds used in hiring labor where there was only one before. So the stoppage of unproductive consumption has benefited labor. Therefore, unproductive consumption hurts labor.

PROPOSITION X.

The division of labor increases its efficiency.

It would be a waste of labor and time for the farmer, after having harvested his wheat, to carry it to the mill, grind it himself into flour, take the flour to the city, then bake it into bread, and then carry the loaf around in search of a buyer for it. The farmer knows how to farm and has the needed tools. He does not know how to run a mill, or a railroad, or a bakery, and he has none of the necessary machinery. His labor can therefore be best used on the farm. If he can earn $5 by working five days, one as a farmer, one as a miller, one as a carrier, one as a baker, and one as a peddler, his labor during the same five days on the farm would probably be worth two or three times that sum. Moreover, if he confines himself to farming, he has to buy only one set of tools and can keep them almost constantly in use, so that his capital does not lie idle. If he pursued five trades, he would have to have five different sets of tools, and four sets would have to lie idle all the while. Therefore, both capital and labor can be best employed where labor is divided.

This is true also within the limits of one trade. Adam Smith, the first great politico-economist, gives the following illustration of the efficiency produced by the division of labor: " The business of making a pin is divided into about eighteen distinct operations. One man draws out the wire, another straights it, a third cuts it, a fourth points it, a fifth grinds it at the top for receiving the head; to make the head requires two or three distinct operations; to put it on is a peculiar business; to whiten the pins is another; it is even a trade by itself to put them into the paper. I have seen a small manufactory where ten men only were employed, and where some of them consequently performed two or three distinct operations. But though they were very poor, and therefore but indifferently accommodated with the necessary machinery, they could, when they exerted themselves, make among them about twelve pounds of pins in a day. There are in a pound upwards of four thousand pins of a middling size. Those ten persons, therefore, could make among them upwards of forty-eight thousand pins in a day. Each person, therefore, making a tenth part of forty-eight thousand pins, might be considered as making four thousand eight hundred pins in a day. But if they had all wrought separately and independently, and without any of them being educated to this peculiar business, they certainly could not each of them have made twenty, perhaps not one, pin in a day."

There are five reasons why the division of labor increases its efficiency.

First, the individual workman acquires more dexterity by doing the same thing many times than by doing many things a few times. A man will be a better blacksmith if he works at that trade every day than if he gives half the week to blacksmithing and half to some other trade;

Second, the time lost by passing from one employment to another is saved by the division of labor. In pin-making, if the man who straightened the wire cut it afterwards, he would have to drop one set of tools and take up another. He might have to move from one part of the shop to another. The time spent in doing so would amount to some days in the course of a year;

Third, it is unnecessary, when labor is properly divided, to buy tools that are used only part of the time. In the case just given, the tools used in straightening the wire would lie idle while the wire was being cut, and *vice versa*. But when two men have charge of these two processes, both sets of tools are used all the while;

Fourth, when labor is divided, the light parts can be given to weak persons, such as women and children, and the heavy parts to strong men. Thus each employé can be given the work best suited to his or her powers;

Fifth, when a workman does one thing constantly, he is more apt to invent some new and better method of doing it than he would be were his attention divided among a number of processes.

Labor can be advantageously divided to any extent, as long as each employé has all his time occupied.

There are two disadvantages to the individual laborer in the division of labor. First, his work is more monotonous, and therefore may be less pleasant. Second, he can do only one small thing well, and therefore has more difficulty in finding work when out of employment.

These disadvantages, however, decrease the efficiency of labor very little. The advantages far outweigh them.

Therefore, the division of labor increases its efficiency.

DEFINITION 9. *The part of capital which is, or might be, used to pay labor is called the wage-fund.*

The part which is so used is the real wage fund. The part that might be so used, that is, the part which capitalists could afford to give in exchange for labor, is the possible wage-fund. The distinction is important.

A manufacturer may pay $100,000 a year in wages, and make a profit of $25,000 for himself. Rather than have his capital lie idle, he would probably be willing to pay $110,000 in wages, and clear only $15,000. In this case the real wage-fund is $100,000, and the possible wage-fund is one-tenth more, or $110,000.

The real wage-fund can never exceed the possible one, but it may fall below it. Workmen, through ignorance or lack of combined effort, may receive less than their employers could afford to pay.

PROPOSITION XI.

The possible wage-fund varies with production.

If production increases, the possible wage-fund increases, and *vice versa*.

The wage-fund can never exceed the sum which the capitalist is willing to give in exchange for labor, because he will cease to use his capital rather than expend more than this in wages. But since the wages paid by the capitalist are repaid him by the sale of the product, the more valuable the product is, the more he will be willing to give in exchange for labor.

Therefore, as the product increases in value, the greater will be the possible wage-fund. And as the product decreases in value, the less will be the possible wage-fund.

Suppose a knife-manufacturer pays $1 for labor which produces, in a day, two knives worth $1 a piece. If the workman labors with greater energy or care and so produces $2.50 worth of knives every day, the manufacturer will be willing to pay a higher price for his labor, because it will be worth more than it was before. But if the workman becomes lazy or careless and produces only $1.50 worth of knives every day, the manufacturer cannot afford to pay him as high wages as he did before, and will therefore cut down his wages.

Therefore, the possible wage-fund varies with production.

PROPOSITION XII.

The real wage-fund varies according to the first law of demand and supply.

Wages are the price paid for labor. We have seen (Prop. VI) that prices depend upon the ratio of demand and supply. If demand exceeds supply, prices rise. If supply exceeds demand, prices fall. At any given time, there is a demand for labor, represented by the capital

seeking investment, and a supply of labor, represented
by the men, women and children seeking employment.
The ratio between the two fixes (Prop. VI) the rate of
wages.

For if the capital seeking investment is small, and the
number of people offering their labor is large, the latter
will compete with each other for employment and will be
willing to work for very little rather than get nothing to
do.   Therefore, wages will be low.   If the capital seeking investment is large, and the number of possible
laborers small, the capitalists will compete with each
other for the chance of employing labor, and will be
willing to give high wages rather than have their capital
lie idle.   Therefore, wages will rise.

The reason that wages increase with the skill, morality
and trustworthiness of the individual laborer is that the
demand for such labor is in excess of the supply.

When the Grand Trunk railway was being built in
Canada, English masons were sent to that country.
They had earned 5*s.* a day in England.   For doing the
same work in Canada, they got 7*s.* 6*d.* a day.   It cost
them no more to live in one country than in the other.
The Canada wages were therefore 1½ times as high as
the English wages.   The reason of the difference was
that there was a greater demand for masons, in proportion to the supply of masons, in Canada than in England.

Therefore, the real wage-fund varies according to the
first law of supply and demand.

PROPOSITION XIII.

**Wages are lower in an agreeable than in a disagreeable,
in an easily-learned than in a difficult, and in a steady
than in an unsteady, employment.**

For persons, in choosing their trades and professions,
are apt to take the most agreeable employment, the one
that seems to them easiest to learn, and the one which
apparently offers them the most constant work.   The

result is that the supply of labor in the employments that are disagreeable, hard to learn, and uncertain, is much less than the supply of labor in more favored industries. It is therefore more apt to be insufficient to meet the demand. Consequently (Prop. XII) its wages are apt to be higher.

Scavengers get high wages because their work is very disagreeable; engravers get them because their work is hard to learn; and plumbers get them because their work is very uncertain, now brisk and now dull.

Therefore, wages are lower in an agreeable than in a disagreeable, in an easily-learned than in a difficult, and in a steady than in an unsteady, employment.

PROPOSITION XIV.

The average wage of labor is equal to the quotient got by dividing the real wage-fund by the number of persons employed.

If the daily wage-fund of an employer is $100, and he hires fifty men, it is evident that he must pay them an *average* wage of $2, which is the quotient of the wage-fund ($100) divided by the number of men employed (50). This will be equally true if the wage-fund is that of a country instead of one man, is yearly instead of daily, and is counted by millions instead of tens of dollars, and if the laborers are many thousands instead of few in number. Since the real wage-fund (Def. 9) is the money actually paid to laborers, the part of it paid to each laborer, *on an average*, must be equal to the whole divided by the number of wage-getters.

Therefore, the average wage of labor is equal to the quotient got by dividing the real wage-fund by the number of persons employed.

PROPOSITION XV.

The test of the highness of wages is their purchasing power.

If the wages of A will buy more than the wages of B will, A's wages are higher than those of B, although they may not contain as many dollars and cents. Thus, if A, in New York, gets $3 a day, and B, in California, is paid $4 a day, and if clothing, food, rent, etc., are twice as dear in California as in New York, $3 in New York will buy as much as $6 in California, and therefore A can earn as many necessary things in a day as B can in one and a-half days. Hence A's wages are higher than B's, although he gets $1 less a day.

Suppose John Smith, an English carpenter, earns four shillings ($1) a day, and John Brown, an American, earns $2 a day. Suppose, too, that a suit of clothes costs $6 in England and $15 in America. Then Smith's wages, reckoned in clothes, are larger than Brown's; for Smith can earn a suit in six days, while Brown has to work seven and a-half days in order to earn it. If other necessaries are as cheap in England as clothes are, then Smith's wages, reckoned in anything except money, are larger than Brown's.

To compare wages, then, we must first find out how much money each laborer gets, and then how much that amount of money will buy. The man who can buy the most has really the highest wages, no matter how low they may be in dollars and cents.

Therefore, the test of the highness of wages is their purchasing power.

PROPOSITION XVI.

Wages can be raised only by increasing the real wage-fund or by lessening the number of persons employed.

This is evident, because (Prop. XIV) wages are the quotient of the real wage-fund divided by the number of men employed, and the quotient can be increased only by increasing the dividend, or by diminishing the divisor.

In this case, the dividend may be increased in four ways:

First, when the real wage-fund (see explanation of Def. 9) is the same as the possible wage-fund, an increase in production may be caused by increased energy on the part of the laborers. This (Prop. XI) will increase the possible wage-fund. The laborers can then persuade, or perhaps by united action compel, the employer to advance the real wage-fund as far as the possible wage-fund has advanced. Suppose a farmer can afford to use four-tenths of his annual crop in paying his laborers, and does so. If the crop is worth $100, the laborers will get $40. If the crop rises in value to $200, the possible wage-fund will be $80. The laborers may be able to persuade the farmer to give them the benefit of this advance. If not, they can compel him to do so by refusing to work except for the increased pay; *provided*, that he can get nobody else to take their places. This latter remedy for low wages is, however, a dangerous one for the laborers, as Prop. XIX will show.

Second, when the real wage-fund is below the possible wage-fund, persuasion or compulsion may make it the same.

Third, both the real and the possible wage-funds are increased (Prop. XV) whenever the commodities bought by the laboring classes are cheapened.

Fourth, if a laborer, or anybody else, avoids unproductive consumption and saves what he can, he increases the wealth of the country, therefore the capital, and therefore the wage-fund. It is calculated that every $1,000 in the savings-banks, by being loaned to a man who wishes to use it as capital, can employ one extra laborer.

It is far better to increase the dividend (the real wage-fund) than to diminish the divisor (the number of men employed).

A decrease in this divisor will not always increase the quotient, because it is apt to cause a decrease in the dividend. If a wage-fund of $10 is divided among five men, and the death or idleness of one man involves a decrease of $2 in the wage-fund, wages will remain the same. At first, five men got $10, or $2 apiece, now four men get $8, or $2 apiece. There are two ways in which a decrease in the number of men employed may not increase the wages of the remainder:

First, since capital cannot produce anything (Prop. I) except with the aid of labor, a diminution of the latter may make the stock of capital too large to be profitably used in connection with the labor that is left. Part of it will, therefore, be withdrawn. This will diminish the general wage-fund. This decrease in the dividend may be large enough to balance, or more than balance, the decrease in the divisor. If it just balances it, wages will remain the same, as the last example shows. If it more than balances it, wages will fall. Thus if the withdrawal of one of the five men leads to the reduction of the wage-fund to $7, the four who are left will get only $1.75, instead of $2, apiece. Moreover, the diminished production of one commodity, which is apt to result from the withdrawal of labor, will raise its price, and thus (Prop. XV) really decrease the wages of all buyers of that commodity;

Second, if the men thrown out of work find nothing else to do, they will be unproductive consumers. They will then be supported at the expense of the whole country, including, of course, all wage-getters. This will diminish the wealth of the country. A decrease in wealth usually involves a decrease in capital, and a decrease in capital means a smaller wage-fund. In this case too, then, a smaller divisor will involve a smaller dividend, and therefore the quotient may not be greater.

Lessening the number of men employed is thus at best only a temporary remedy for low wages. By de-creasing the supply, and thus (Prop. VI) raising the price of the commodity on which less labor is now spent, it diminishes the wages of all buyers of that commodity. By causing a direct withdrawal of capital, it diminishes the wage-fund. By increasing the unproductive consumption of the country, it lessens its wealth and therefore its wage-fund.

Nevertheless, this decrease in the number of employees may raise wages. If half the carpenters in this country should die or emigrate, the wages of the other half would be advanced, although, owing to the consequent withdrawa. of some capital, the new wages probably would not be double the old ones.

Therefore, wages can be raised only by increasing the real wage-fund, or by lessening the number of persons employed.

PROPOSITION XVII.

The use of labor-saving machinery benefits labor.

The use of such machinery may at first diminish the number of laborers employed, but it will ultimately increase the number. If a spinning-machine which enables two men to do the work of ten is invented, its use would probably lead, at first, to the discharge of some of the spinners then employed. The saving in labor would make spun goods cheaper. This would (Prop. XV) really raise the wages of all laborers who used such goods. Moreover, the manufacture of the new machines would lead to the employment of more machinists.

The gain, too, would be lasting, while the loss would be only temporary. Experience has shown that an article offered at a low price will be bought by many persons who would prefer to get along without it if the price asked were a little higher. If a manufacturer can produce linen at a cost of 95 cents a yard, and can sell one thousand yards if he asks $1.05 a yard, and three thousand yards if he asks only $1, it will pay him to choose the latter price, because he will then make a larger sum of money.   His two accounts would be as follows:

```
1,000 yards sold at $1.05................................$1,050
Cost of same at 95 cents...............................    950
                                                        ------
    Total profit........... ....................... ....$   100

3,000 yards sold at $1 ................................$3,000
Cost of same at 95 cents ............... .............  2,850
                                                        ------
    Total profit....................................... $   150
```

The extra profit at the lower price is $50.

The great reduction in the cost of production, and therefore in the selling-price of goods made by machinery, has always hitherto so increased the demand for the goods that the manufacturers have ere long employed at least as many workpeople, with the machinery, as they did before the machinery was invented.   Usually they have employed many more.   Thus, to take the case of linen, the persons now employed in its manufacture greatly outnumber those so employed when the work was nearly all done by hand.

The following little table, condensed from Mr. Thomas Brassey's "Work and Wages," p. 125, shows that in England, Scotland and Ireland the number of persons employed in the manufacture of several important commodities has increased with the increase of the number of labor-saving machines, and decreased with the decrease in such machinery:

		1856.	1861.	1868.
Cotton.....	{ Number of power-looms .	298,847	399,992	379,329
	{ Number of employees ...	379,213	451,569	401,064
Woolen, etc.	{ Number of power-looms .	53,399	64,818	118,865
	{ Number of employees ...	166,885	173,046	253,056
Flax, etc....	{ Number of power-looms .	8,689	15,347	35,047
	{ Number of employees ...	80,262	94,003	135,333

The temporary loss of employment by the people whose labor is done by machinery is more than counterbalanced by the permanent gain of the people whose labor is necessary to make the machines and by the finally increased demand for the labor temporarily injured. Besides this, the increased cheapness of the machine-made goods (Prop. XV) raises the wages of every laborer who buys them. This is a permanent gain in most cases for all laborers.

Therefore, the use of labor-saving machinery benefits labor.

PROPOSITION XVIII.

High wages often make high profits.

The cost of labor "is determined by the amount of work really done for the wages."* Thus, if A and B are paid equal wages, and A does twice as much work as B, B's labor is twice as dear as A's. Suppose they get $2 apiece. B produces 10 yards of linen in a day and A produces 20 yards. Each yard produced by B therefore costs 20 cents for labor, while each produced by A costs only 10 cents for labor. It will be cheaper for the employer to hire A at $3 a day than to continue to employ B at $2. For then linen will still cost ($3 ÷ 20 =) only 15 cents a yard for labor, whereas with B at $2 it will cost 20 cents a yard for labor. Good labor at good wages may therefore be cheaper than poor labor at poor wages.

If an employer gives higher wages than his neighbors, he will attract to his service the very best laborers. He will therefore have the advantage of a set of workmen who have more strength, skill, carefulness, economy in the use of materials, honesty, and sobriety, than those of his neighbors. His employees will be careful not to lose their good places by quarreling with him in any way. The feeling that he is treating them generously will lead them to treat him in the same way. They will not shirk work, and thus part of the expense of overseers may be

* Prof. Fawcett.

saved. The cheerfulness and hopefulness caused by their improved material condition will increase their productive powers. In Austria free hired labor was found to be three times as productive as the labor of serfs. The better food which men getting higher wages can buy may also increase their powers of production.

Thus high wages tend to increase production. They often, as experience has shown, increase it so largely that the real cost of production is less, and the profits are therefore higher.

The following proofs of this are taken from Mr. Thomas Brassey's "Work and Wages":

"At the commencement of the construction of the North Devon [Eng.] railway, the wages of the laborers were 2s. a day. During the progress of the work their wages were raised to 2s. 6d. and 3s. a day. Nevertheless, it was found that the work was executed more cheaply when the men were earning the higher rate of wages than when they were paid at the lower rate.

"In London, in carrying out part of the Metropolitan Drainage works, it was found that the brickwork was constructed at a cheaper rate per cubic yard after the wages of the workmen had been raised to 10s., than when they were paid at the rate of 6s. a day.

"In the same quarry at Bonnières [France], in which Frenchmen, Irishmen and Englishmen were employed side by side, the Frenchmen received 3 francs, the Irishmen 4, and the Englishmen 6 francs a day. At those different rates, the Englishman was found to be the most advantageous workman of the three.

"During the construction of the refreshment-room at Basingsbroke [Eng.], on one side of the station a London bricklayer was employed at 5s. 6d. a day, and on the other two country bricklayers at 3s. 6d. apiece a day. It was found, by measuring the work performed, without the knowledge of the men employed, that the one London bricklayer laid, without undue exertion, more bricks in a day than his two less skilful country fellow-laborers.

"On the Grand Trunk railway, a number of French Canadian laborers were employed. Their wages were 3s. 6d. a day, while the Englishmen received from 5s. to 6s. a day; but it was found that the English did the greatest amount of work for the money."

If high wages incite men to better work, a smaller number of men can be employed to produce a given amount. In this way, while the wages of the individual are higher, the aggregate wages (the real wage-fund) may be less. If 10 men, getting $3 a day, will do the work of 16 men, who get $2 a day, it is manifestly cheaper for the employer to hire the 10 men. For then he will pay only $30 a day in wages instead of $32, and will still have the same product.

The French smelting-works employ 42 men to do the work done by 25 men in English works of the same sort. If the Frenchmen get $1 a day, and the Englishmen $1.50, the real cost of labor is greater in France than in England; for the 42 men will be paid $42 a day, and the 25 men $37.50 a day. Both sets do the same work. Therefore the labor on this work costs $4.50 less in England than in France.

It must be remembered that increased wages can only make increased profits by increasing production. Hence, if men are not induced to work better by getting better wages, it is bad policy for the employer to give such wages. There are cases in which high wages will not stimulate production. When the laborer can buy all he needs with low wages, if wages rise, he will labor just long enough to earn what he used to earn in a day, and will idle away the rest of his time. The Hindoos employed in railway-building in India worked less and less as their wages rose. The coal-miners in England have had their wages greatly increased since 1870, but their hours of work have since been fewer, so that the value of the coal produced has not kept pace with the increased value of the wages. Their high wages have

3

therefore diminished, not increased, profits. These cases show that high wages do not always make high profits. The previous proof, however, has shown that they sometimes do, and in fact are apt to do so.

Therefore, high wages often make high profits.

DEFINITION 10. *A strike is a conspiracy of employees against employers, by which the former refuse to work unless the latter yield to their wishe*

DEFINITION 11. *A lock-out is a conspiracy of employers against employees, by which the former refuse to give the latter work unless the employees yield to their wishes.*

PROPOSITION XIX.

It is bad policy to strike.

When men strike, the side which can afford to be idle the longest will win. The masters are usually rich enough to live on their accumulated property for some time. The men often have no savings, and rarely, if ever, have large ones. They may belong to a trade-union which will supply them with means of subsistence for some time, but the small funds of such a society, divided among a number of men, cannot go far. The masters must have the men work in order to have their capital yield them anything, but the men must work in order to live. It is plain that the masters can, as a rule, stay idle the longest.

The masters can combine against the men. Since a strike which forced one employer to raise wages would probably compel all similar employers in that part of the country to increase their wage-funds, too, it is to the apparent interest of every employer that no strike should succeed. Hence, if one set of employees is supported while on strike by the contributions of their comrades who are still at work, the employers of the latter often make a lock-out (Def. 11), and so cut off this source of supply and starve all the men together into submission.

The masters can combine with more effect than the men, because they are fewer and better informed.

It grows more difficult to strike successfully, every year, because the increased facilities of transportation enable the employers to bring men from other parts of the country, and even from other countries, to take the place of the strikers. Men have been engaged in Sweden and brought to this country to take the place of Americans who were on strike.

A strike is apt to create a habit of idleness among the strikers, which unfits them for good work thereafter. They are often led to drink in order to while away the time. The want from which they and their families suffer while they earn nothing, sometimes drives them to theft. If these dangers are escaped, a strike usually consumes all the men's savings, and obliges them to waste, in unproductive consumption, a large part, if not all, of the trade-union's funds, which are the joint savings of themselves and their fellows. The strike of the Preston (England) spinners, in 1836, cost, the men $300,000 and the masters over $200,000. The strike of 17,000 Preston spinners for thirty-six weeks, in 1853, cost the masters $825,000 and the men $2,100,000. The strike of the Belfast (Ireland) weavers in 1874 cost the strikers $1,000,000.

The fear of constant trouble from strikes is apt to drive away capital, and thus make it necessary for the men dependent upon the wage-fund part of that capital to seek employment elsewhere. A prolonged strike has sometimes utterly ruined the industries of a whole town. The prosperity of Norwich, England, ended with a great strike there in 1830.

Much of the Russian trade has been lost to English manufacturers, because the Russian merchants, hearing of strikes in England, and fearing their orders could not be executed there, have sent the orders elsewhere.

If, however, all these obstacles are overcome and the strike succeeds, it very seldom repays the men what they have given for it. They rarely get the higher wages for any long time, unless the working of the first law of supply and demand (Prop. VI) would have soon given them these wages without a strike. For such artificial changes in wages only interrupt, not destroy, the natural law laid down in Proposition XII. Despite all that employers or employees can do, that law will in the long run fix wages.

Suppose 1,000 men, each earning $3 a day or $3,000 a day together, strike for three months in order to get $3.50 a day. The strike will cost them the wages they would have earned, or $3,000 a day. Its total cost for the eighty working days in the three months will be eighty times $3,000 or $240,000. When they resume work at $3.50 a day, they will receive fifty cents apiece, or $500 together a day more than before. This is what the strike pays them. It will be necessary for them to work 480 days (or, including Sundays, over eighteen months) before they have made up the money they lost by the strike; for the loss was $240,000, and $500 a day for 480 days just equals $240,000. Not until the eighteen months are over will the successful strike have added a cent to their incomes. But it is very improbable that they will get the $3.50 for eighteen months, unless the law of wages would, before the eighteen months were over, have given it to them at any rate. And in that event the money spent on the strike was simply wasted.

In order that a strike shall succeed, three things are absolutely necessary: First, the real wage-fund must be less than the possible wage-fund; for if the two coincide, no power whatever (see proof of Prop. XI) can raise wages; second, the men must have means of subsistence for some time; third, they must not only stop work themselves, but they must persuade or compel all their fellow-workmen to refuse to work for this particular employer. If they compel them to refuse, they are liable to be fined or imprisoned; for a man has a right to sell his labor to anybody engaged in honest business, and compelling him to give up this right is a crime.

While, then, a strike may sometimes succeed, the chances are greatly against it; and if it does succeed, it rarely repays its cost.

Therefore, it is bad policy to strike.

PROPOSITION XX.

It is to the advantage of both employers and employees to settle their disputes by arbitration.

This method of settlement is as follows: The employers and the employees together choose one or more persons who are to act as the judge or judges of the dispute. Before the court thus formed each side states its grievances and its wishes. The workmen explain, for instance, why they think their wages should be increased, and the employers tell what reasons they have for not raising wages. The judges, having heard both sides fully, decide which is right.

As the judges are chosen for their integrity and fairness by both the parties to the quarrel, this decision usually satisfies both sides. As masters and men agreed to submit the question to these judges, both parties are bound, in honor, to obey the decision that is given. They usually do so. Thus an interruption of work and a waste of wealth by a strike or a lock-out are prevented, and good feeling is preserved between masters and men.

Mr. Walter Morrison, a Member of Parliament, and Judge Rupert Kettle, both of England, have persuaded the employers and employees in a number of English manufacturing towns to establish permanent boards of arbitration. Half of the members of these boards are elected by the masters, and half by the men. They have decided very many trade disputes, and have saved millions of dollars that would have been wasted if the men interested had struck against the masters, or if the masters had locked-out the men.

In France, there are regular arbitration courts (called "Conseils des Prud'hommes"), organized under the laws of the country. These courts consist of a President and Vice-President, appointed by the government, and six other persons, who are elected by the employers and employees. No salaries are paid, so that arbitration is cheap. A committee of the judges, consisting of one employer and one workman, holds almost daily sessions. Thomas Brassey says in his "Work and Wages": "The result in 95 out of 100 cases brought before these tribunals is a reconciliation between the parties, and although appeals are permitted to the superior courts of law they are rarely made. Lord Brougham, in a speech in the House of Lords in 1859, declared that 'in 1850, 28,000 disputes had been heard before the Conseils des Prud'hommes, of which no less than 26,800 were satisfactorily settled.'"

Arbitration has often prevented wasteful strikes and lock-outs in this country.

Therefore, it is to the advantage of both employers and employees to settle their disputes by arbitration.

PROPOSITION XXI.

The best way to produce wealth is by co-operation.

True coöperation exists only when every one who has contributed to the production of anything receives a share of its proceeds in proportion to the worth of his work. If his capital or his labor has done half the work, he owns half the product. If he has done $\frac{1}{1000000}$th part of the work, he owns $\frac{1}{1000000}$th part of the product.

Coöperation may be productive or distributive. It may be between a master and his men, or between the men alone. A coöperative coal-mining company is an example of coöperative production. A coöperative grocery is an example of coöperative distribution. Coöperation between master and men exists when the men

have a share in the profits, outside of their wages. Coöperation between men exists when the men have all the
profits, that is, when the workmen in an establishment
own the establishment between them.
Distributive coöperation is safer than productive.
The capital and skill required in the management of a
grocery, which usually has a steady circle of customers
and sells to-day what it bought yesterday, are much less
than the skill and capital required in the management of
a coal-mine. The cost of mining the coal is great. A
good deal of capital is therefore necessary. The cost is
also rather uncertain. The price at which the product
can be sold varies from week to week. A great number
of causes affect it. All these things must be foreseen, as
far as possible. Great skill is therefore required.
The best of all forms of coöperation is that between
master and men. For in this the men gain the use of
the skill and the capital of the master, and the master
gains the hearty goodwill and the uttermost skill and energy of the men.
There is little coöperation in America, but a good deal
of it in England and Germany.
As an example of coöperative distribution, by workmen alone, we will take the Equitable Pioneer Society,
of Rochdale, a manufacturing town near Manchester,
England. In 1842, twenty-eight weavers formed this
company. They were so poor that they could pay into
the capital-fund only four cents apiece per week. It
took them two years to accumulate a capital of $140.
On a December evening, in 1844, "Toad lane," a dingy
little street in Rochdale, was crowded with a hooting
rabble, gathered to see the opening of the "weavers'
shop." When the shutters of the little room the Society
had hired were taken down, the jeering crowd screamed
with laughter at the sight of the almost empty shelves
within. For a long time the twenty-eight weavers were
the only customers. They could not afford to hire a
clerk, so they took turns in "keeping store" in the even-

ings. It was shut during the day. The scanty stock of groceries was soon sold. Its proceeds bought a larger stock. This went, and the next, and the next, and so on. By buying their goods directly from the producers, they got them so cheaply that they could sell them below the usual prices, pay all the store expenses, and declare a small dividend on the capital. In 1845 their capital-fund was $910. Their membership was seventy-four. Soon they rented a larger room and hired a manager. In 1846, they began to sell meat; in 1847, dry goods; in 1852, boots, shoes and clothing. In 1852 they opened a wholesale department. From the start, the weavers have kept on weaving. This co-operative store is managed by persons they employ, but it does not interfere with their work.

The main building of the Society is now the most conspicuous structure in Rochdale. Its top-floor is a plain, comfortable hall, where the monthly meetings of members are held, lectures delivered, and parties given. On the floor below are the reading-room and the library. The latter has about ten thousand volumes. There are eleven branch reading-rooms in the town. The Society maintains schools for its members and their children. ·It has a collection of scientific instruments which it loans for two or three cents an evening to members who wish them for their own instruction or for the entertainment of their friends. The two lower floors of the building are divided into the different stores the Society owns, and the basement is devoted to packing and storage. There are branch stores in different parts of the town,— among them eleven butcher-shops and thirteen groceries. The Society manufactures tobacco, and has invested some of its spare funds in corn, cotton and woolen mills. These are properly examples of productive co-operation, however, so that we will not discuss them here. In December, 1871, the Society began to build homes for its members. It now sells them coal. Almost from the beginning, it has been their savings bank, receiving deposits at any time and paying interest upon them.

Mr. George Jacob Holyoake, an English journalist, scholar and co-operator, has written a "History of Co-operation in Rochdale." We quote this passge from it :

"These crowds of humble workingmen, who never knew before when they put good food in their mouths, whose every dinner was adulterated, whose shoes let in the water a month too soon, whose new coats shone with 'devil's dust,' and whose wives wore calicoes that would not wash, now buy in the markets like millionaires, and, as far as pureness of food goes, live like lords. They are weaving their own stuffs, making their own shoes, sewing their own garments, grinding their own corn. They buy the purest sugar and the best tea, and grind their own coffee. They slaughter their own cattle, and the finest beasts of the land waddle down the streets of Rochdale for the consumption of flannel-weavers and cobblers. . . . The teetotalers of Rochdale acknowledge that the Store has made more sober men since it commenced than all their efforts have been able to make in the same time. Husbands who never knew what it was to be out of debt, and poor wives who during forty years never had sixpence uncondemned in their pockets, now possess little stores of money, sufficient to build them cottages, and go every week into their own market, with money jingling in their pockets. And in that market there is no distrust and no deception; there is no adulteration and no second prices. The whole atmosphere is honest."

The official report of the Society for the three months ending June 10, 1873, states the amount of sales for that time at $360,985. This enormous business has been built up, and is now controlled, by men who work for daily or weekly wages.

The Equitable Pioneers' Society is organized in this way : Anybody who is approved by a majority of the Executive Committee and of the members can join the Society. He must subscribe for five shares of $5 each, pay an admission fee of 25 cents, and pay 9 cents a week until his five shares are all paid for. The money received in this way is the share-capital of the Society. There is also a loan-capital, formed by deposits by members. Interest is paid on these deposits and they can be withdrawn at any time. While the Society has them, it uses them to extend its business. They are, therefore, part of its capital. All goods are bought and sold for cash.

This rule is not proved by its exceptions, because it has no exceptions whatever. ' The Society sells its wares at about the market rates, sometimes a trifle lower. The profits are divided in this way: The expenses of management and the guaranteed interest of 5 per cent. on the loan-capital are paid; then a dividend (never above 5 per cent.) on the share-capital is declared; then 2½ per cent. of the remainder is allotted to the educational fund (this amounts to over $5,000 a year) ; and the rest is divided among all the patrons of the Store *in proportion to their purchases.* If one person has bought $20 worth of goods, and another $10 worth, the first gets twice as much of this dividend on purchases as the second. A non-member gets about half as much as a member would. In the quarter ending June 10, 1873, the dividend on purchases was 12½ per cent. A member who had bought $100 worth of goods would then get $12.50 back, and a non-member who had bought as largely would get $6.25.

The members of the Equitable Pioneers' Society therefore get back part of the price they pay for everything at their store, get dividends on their shares, get interest on any savings they deposit with the Society, have the use of reading-rooms, books, schools, etc., and get pure, good, unadulterated wares. Adulteration can be prevented only by making the interests of buyer and seller identical, and this can be done only by distributive co-operation.

As an example of co-operative production by employers and workmen together, we will take the Briggs Brothers' Coal-mining Company, in Yorkshire, England.

The Briggs brothers owned and worked two collieries. They were in constant trouble with their men, who were a drinking, uproarious, careless set. The men had a rough saying, "All coal-owners is devils, but Briggs is the prince of devils." This shows how great the ill-feeling was. Strikes were frequent. The men took holidays, too, on the slightest pretext. A boy, by tossing up his cap and shouting "Let's stop work for to-day!" could, it is said, induce the whole crowd of boys and men to spend the day idly. The cost of taking care of the two mines, pumping the water out of them, etc., was $1,000 a day, whether mining was carried on or not. Every day, then, that the men did not work was a clear loss of at least $1,000 to the Briggs brothers. They only made about 6 per cent. on their capital on an average.

In 1860, Prof. Fawcett, a great English statesman and politico-economist, published a sketch of a plan for co-operation between masters and men. In 1866 the Briggs brothers resolved to try this plan. They formed a joint-stock company and issued 9,770 shares, worth $50 each. The men were allowed to buy some of these shares, paying for them in installments. Very few of them have done this, however. Only 264 shares are now held by the workmen. At the same time the Briggs brothers announced that the profits would thereafter be divided in the following way: First, a dividend of 10 per cent. would be paid on all the shares; second, the remainder of the profits would be divided into two equal parts. One of these parts would be used to pay an extra dividend on the capital stock, and the other would be divided among all the workmen, whether shareholders or not, in proportion to the wages each had earned during the year. If A had earned $200 and B $100 during the year, A would get twice as much as B of this dividend on labor.

The results of this were remarkable. The men, having a promise of half the profits over 10 per cent. on the stock, did all they could to raise the profits above that figure. They worked steadily. They were careful of the wood and tools used. When a man found a broken tool, or anything of the sort, instead of kicking it aside as he would once have done, he picked it up and took it to the office to be repaired, saying "That's so much towards the 'divvy.'" "Divvy" is their pet name for dividend. It became the interest of all that each should

work. They acted as overseers for each other. This
saved a good deal. Public opinion, which before favored
dissipation, now opposed it. Idleness, drinking and riot-
ing were frowned upon. They became far less common. The best of good feeling sprang up between the
Briggs brothers and their men. All questions about
wages, hours of work, etc., were settled by friendly talks
or by arbitration. At the end of the first year, under
the new scheme, the Briggs brothers and the sharehold-
ing workmen got a dividend of 10 per cent. and $8,500
besides, while another $8,500 was divided among the
workmen. The second year, the dividend to labor was
$17,500. The plan has now (1875) been in operation
about eight years. The Briggs brothers, who, before
1866–7, got an annual profit of 6 per cent. on their capital, are said to have cleared a yearly profit of from 15 to
17 per cent. ever since. Meanwhile, their workmen,
whether shareholders or not, have had annual dividends
on their labor, and part of the profits have been used in
supporting a library and schools for the benefit of the
miners and their families. There has been a very
noticeable advance in the morality, intelligence and
thrift of the whole body of employees.*

Co-operation thus prevents strikes, promotes good-will,
causes honest work, checks wastefulness, saves the expense of overseers, offers the workman an opportunity to
invest his savings at a profit, encourages thrift, morality
and education, and increases the profits of all the co-
operators.†

Therefore, the best way to produce wealth is by
co-operation.

* Since this passage was written, a trade-union to which the miners employed
by the Briggs brothers belonged has compelled them to break up this industrial
partnership. This action on the part of the union was a piece of barbarous
stupidity, without excuse. The reason for it is unknown.

† Mr. Charles Bradlaugh informs us that in his opinion distributive co-
operation has been *proved* a complete success in England, and that productive co-operation, although tried as yet only in a few cases, promises well.

PROPOSITION XXII.

Trade-union funds can be best used in promoting co-operation.

These funds are now used in two ways. First, in helping members of the particular union to live while they cannot find work, and in making up their losses by fire, theft, etc. Second, in supporting them while on strike. The first use is a good one. The second is apt (Prop. XIX) to merely waste the funds. It is rarely advisable. The wealth wasted in supporting a set of strikers for some weeks or months would often be more than enough, if loaned to the men by the union, to enable them to buy an interest in their employer's business, or even to set them up in business for themselves.

In 1874, the journeymen shoemakers of Chicago, after a long and useless strike against a reduction of wages, started a co-operative shoe-manufactory. It failed for want of capital. But the wealth furnished by the trade-union and unproductively consumed by the shoemakers while on strike would have been more than enough capital for their manufactory. If it had been loaned to them for this purpose at the beginning, and if any of them had had sufficient skill to manage the business, they could have had both the wages of their labor and the profits on it for themselves. As it was, they consumed the wealth unproductively, cleared no profit on it, and had to go back to work at the lower rates offered by their old employers. Some of them could not get work at all, because the vacant places had been partly filled with shoemakers brought from the East. These unfortunates had to go to the expense of seeking employment in other cities.

Trade-unions should use their funds in this way. As soon as a union accumulates a few hundred or thousand dollars above the amount it needs for the relief of temporary distress among its members, it should loan this surplus, with proper precautions for its repayment, to the set of its members which would pay most for the use of it. These men should then employ it in productive or distributive co-operation. By the former they could raise their wages in money, and so in purchasing power. By the latter, they could raise them in purchasing power by cheapening the prices of the necessaries of life. They would gradually repay the loan out of their extra profits. Meanwhile, the trade-union would accumulate another surplus, and loan that in the same way. This would be repeated again and again, until at length all the members of the union would become small capitalists as well as laborers, getting profits on their capital and wages on their labor.

At present, trade-union funds do only temporary good to the members of the union. Under the system here proposed, the funds would do the members permanent good.

Therefore, trade-union funds can be best used in promoting co-operation.

PROPOSITION XXIII.

Wealth, when produced, is divided into rent, profits and wages.

We have seen (Prop. I) that three things are needed to produce wealth,—natural agents, capital and labor. Each of the three must be paid for, except (Prop. II) the natural agents which are practically unlimited in quantity, and therefore are not wealth. Rent* is the portion of the product which pays for the limited natural agents; profits, the portion which pays for the capital; and wages, the portion which pays for the labor.

Suppose A rents an iron-mine and the land on which his smelting works stand for $10,000 a year. He pays wages of $70,000 a year. The annual product of his works is 100,000 bars of iron worth $1 apiece. Then

* Notice the difference between this meaning of "rent" and its ordinary meaning.

the $100,000 of wealth produced will be divided into rent of $10,000, wages of $70,000 and profits of $20,000. If A has had charge of the business, the $20,000 will be partly profits, and partly his wages as general manager.

The real profits are usually smaller than the apparent ones, because the portion of the product allotted to the capitalist is usually partly composed of his wages. His mental labor has as much right to reward as the mental or bodily labor of his employees. It is not correct to include the wages he earns in the profits his capital earns.

Since there can be no production (Prop. 1) if any one of the three factors does not aid the other two, it is right that every one of the three should be rewarded for its aid. Thus capital has as much right to its profits as labor has to its wages.

The limited natural agents, capital and labor, are all wealth. Therefore (Def. 4) something can be got in exchange for them. And hence, since all three are used in producing wealth, the owners of each get something in exchange for it from the wealth produced.

Therefore, wealth, when produced, is divided into rent, profits and wages.

PROPOSITION XXIV.

Wealth is sometimes shared between three classes, and sometimes between two, and is sometimes absorbed by one.

When the land, the capital and the labor used in production are furnished by three different persons, or sets of persons, the first gets the rent, the second the profits, and the third the wages.

But when one class furnishes any two of these three productive powers, the wealth is shared between two classes. For if one man owns the land and the capital, he gets both the rent and the profits. The other persons, who furnish the labor, get the wages. If some agricultural laborers rent a farm and cultivate it, they will get the profits and wages, and the landowner will get the rent. If a landowner borrows some capital to use on his land and does the necessary work himself, he will get the rent and the wages, and the part of the profits earned by his capital, and the lender of the rest of the capital will get the rest of the profits.

When one man owns the land, the capital and the labor (his own or that of slaves), he gets rent, profits, and wages. A market-gardener may own a piece of land and the capital used in cultivating it, and may do all the necessary work himself. Then he gets rent, profits and wages. That is, all the wealth produced by his land, his capital and his labor belongs to him.

Therefore, wealth is sometimes shared between three classes, and sometimes between two, and is sometimes absorbed by one.

PROPOSITION XXV.

The first law of supply and demand fixes the proportion of rent, profits and wages to each other.

If there is a great deal of land seeking employment and a comparatively small demand for land, then (Prop. VI) the price paid for its use will be small, and therefore the rent will take but a small part of the product. If the supply of land does not equal the demand for it, then (Prop. VI) the rent will be a larger part of the product.

In the same way, the ratio of demand to supply will decide what part of the product shall be used to pay profits, and what part to pay wages.

Therefore, the first law of supply and demand fixes the proportion of rent, profits and wages to each other.

DEFINITION 12. *Value is purchasing power.*

The value of a thing is its power of purchasing other things. If a yard of velvet will buy two yards of broadcloth, or three yards of linen, the value of velvet is twice that of broadcloth and thrice that of linen. If a pound of tea will exchange for three pounds of coffee, the value of tea is thrice that of coffee.

The value of a thing is always found by comparing it with other things.

DEFINITION 13. *Price is value expressed in money.*

For the sake of convenience, one universal standard of value has been taken. This standard is money. It is a common denominator of values. Instead of saying that the value of a pound of tea is three times the value of a pound of coffee, we say that tea is worth 90 cents and coffee 30 cents a pound.

When the value of a thing is expressed in money, it is called its price.

PROPOSITION XXVI.

There cannot be a general rise or fall in values.

Suppose there were only two things in the world, one named A and the other B. There could not be a general rise in their value. For the value of a thing (Def. 12) is its power of purchasing other things. If A rises in value, it must buy more of B. Then it will take more of B to buy A. B's value will therefore be less. Thus, if A rises in value, B must fall in value. And if B rises in value, it must buy more of A. That is, A must fall in value. Since each must fall in order that the other may rise, in value, they cannot rise together.

What is thus true of two things is equally true of three, four and all things. In order that one may rise in value, others must fall. And so, if one falls in value, others must rise. For the one will then have less purchasing power. That is, it will buy less of other commodities. The others, then, will buy more of it. They will therefore have more value.

Suppose one pound of tea will buy three pounds of coffee or four pounds of sugar. Their values, compared with each other, cannot all rise together ; for if tea grows so dear that one pound of it will buy four pounds of coffee or five pounds of sugar, then the value of coffee

4

and sugar has fallen.   It takes more of each of them to
buy a pound of tea.

Thus, in order that one thing may rise in value, others
must fall.   And *vice versa.*

Therefore, there cannot be a general rise or fall in
values.

PROPOSITION XXVII.

There may be a general rise or fall in prices.

One thing may rise in value, but in order that it may
do so, other things (Prop. XXVI) must fall.   If money
rises in value, it will take less of it to buy other commodities.   Therefore, general prices will fall.   If money
falls in value, it will take more of it to buy other commodities.   Therefore, general prices will rise.

If tea has been selling for 90 cents, coffee for 30, and
sugar for 22½, a pound, and a scanty supply (Prop. VI)
forces their prices up to $1.80, 60 and 45 cents a pound,
the value of money, so far as they are concerned, will
have fallen.   A dollar will not exchange for as much of
them as it used to.   There has been a general rise in
their prices, but there has been neither rise nor fall in
their values, compared with each other.   For a pound of
tea, before the rise in price, would have bought three
pounds of coffee or four of sugar, and it will buy pre-
cisely the same amount now.

Therefore, there may be a general rise or fall in
prices.

PROPOSITION XXVIII.

The value of a thing depends upon the cost of its production.

No commodity will be produced unless there is a demand (Def. 6) for it.   Neither will a commodity be produced unless those who want it are willing to give in
exchange for it something of equal value.   For, since it

always costs something to produce a commodity, the producer will not be willing to exchange it for less than it cost him. This cost is called the cost of production. Since the article will not be exchanged for less than its cost of production, its value (Def. 12) must depend upon this.

The cost of production consists of the limited natural agents used up, the mental and bodily labor expended, and the capital consumed, in the production. Both the labor and the wages paid for it are to be reckoned, for the first is the sacrifice or cost of the laborer, and the second is part of the sacrifice or cost of the capitalist.

The cost of production fixes the *intrinsic* value, that is, the value at which the article can be exchanged without loss. Its *market* value is somewhat greater than this, because the capitalist sells it at a profit. If he made no profit, he would not care to use his capital in producing the commodity.

Intrinsic value is fixed. Market value varies with supply and demand (Prop. VI). It may sometimes even fall below intrinsic value, but if it does so for any length of time, production (Prop. VII) will slacken and the consequent diminished supply (Prop. VI) will send up the market value again.

Therefore, the value of a thing depends upon the cost of its production.

PROPOSITION XXIX.

In every fair bargain, both parties gain.

One man's gain cannot be another man's loss, in trade, except in cases of ignorance or deceit.

If a man in England exchanges steel for cotton with a man in America, each is a gainer. The value of the steel is equal to the value of the cotton, or the exchange would not be made. Each now has what he wants, whereas each before had what he wanted to part with.

The Englishman wanted the cotton more than he did the steel. The American wanted the steel more than he did the cotton. Each has his greater want gratified. So both have gained.

What is true of the Englishman and the American is true of the New York merchant and the Iowa farmer, or of a million Englishmen and a million Americans.

Therefore, in every fair bargain, both parties gain.

PROPOSITION XXX.

The first method of exchange, barter, is unfit for use in a civilized community.

Barter is the exchange of one thing for another without the use of money. This was the first method of exchange. It is the way in which all buying and selling is still carried on in some barbarous communities. If a savage has more food than he can eat, he exchanges the surplus for something he needs,—a skin or a bow and arrows.

This method of exchange is inconvenient. It would not be practicable among civilized people.

A tailor has only clothes to sell. If he wanted a loaf of bread and barter still prevailed, he would have to offer a baker some article of clothing, a coat for instance, in exchange for bread. But probably the baker would have all the coats he needed. He might say he wanted a stove. Then the tailor would have to find a stove-maker who was willing to exchange a stove for a coat; get a stove in this way; and then give the baker the stove for the bread. If he could find no such stove-maker, he would have to hunt for another baker. "He might starve before he could find any person having bread to sell who wanted a coat; besides, he would not want as much bread at a time as would be worth a coat, and the coat could not be divided." *

* John Stuart Mill.

What is true of the exchange between the tailor and the baker is true of all other exchanges. It is easy to see, then, that barter hinders trade.

Therefore, the first method of exchange, barter, is unfit for use in a civilized community.

PROPOSITION XXXI.

The great instrument of exchange is money.

The impossibility of carrying on trade in civilized countries by barter made the introduction of money a necessity. Money is the great medium of exchange. Whoever has enough money can buy whatever is offered for sale.

The tailor mentioned in the last proposition could get the bread he wanted of the baker if he had money. It is by means of money that the lawyer exchanges his legal ability for his food, clothing, rent, etc., and that a teacher exchanges his learning for rent, groceries, clothes, etc. The teacher first sells his learning for money, and then he sells his money for groceries, clothes, fuel, the use of a house, etc.

The same thing is true of all civilized men. Take the case of a shoe-dealer. His wealth is in shoes. Through the medium of money, he exchanges his shoes for whatever he wants. He sells his shoes for money, and then sells the money for leather, or bread, or a ticket to a concert, or anything else.

Therefore, the great instrument of exchange is money.

PROPOSITION XXXII.

Money is the measure of values.

Lengths are measured by inches, feet, yards, etc.; weights by ounces, pounds, etc.; time by minutes, hours, days, and years; and values are measured by money.

Money may therefore be defined as the medium of exchange and the measure of values.

If there were no measure of values, it would be difficult to tell at any time how much of one commodity
should be given in exchange for another.   It would be
impossible to know how much any man was worth without naming all the things he owned, one after another.

When the tailor wishes to let his customer know the
value of a coat, he expresses that value in money.   When
a man wishes to tell how rich he is, he expresses it in
money, too.

Therefore, money is the measure of values.

PROPOSITION XXXIII.

Money in specie is like all other commodities.

Money in specie is gold or silver money.   Paper
money is not specie.   Specie money is a commodity like all
other commodities.   Gold and silver, whether coined or
not, are commodities, just as iron and lead are.

The value of specie depends upon the cost of production, as the value of all other commodities does.
The value of specie money is the value of the metal com-
posing it, and the cost of coining it.   The value of the
metal depends upon the cost of producing it, that is, the
cost of getting it out of the mine and of freeing it from
impurities.

The value of specie is affected by demand and supply,
just as all other values are.   If the stock of gold greatly
increases, an ounce of gold will exchange for less food,
clothes, or anything else.   If the stock of gold decreases,
an ounce of it will exchange for more food, clothing, etc.

All the other natural laws affecting commodities
apply to gold and silver.

Therefore, money *in specie* is like all other commodities.

PROPOSITION XXXIV.

Gold and silver make the best money.

The thing which is to serve as money should —

(1) have large value in small space and weight, because otherwise nobody could carry about with him enough to buy what he needed, from time to time; and if he bought on credit, much time and labor would have to be spent in finally taking a large, heavy substance to the stores in settlement of the bills;

(2) be steady in value, because something which changes its own value continually cannot measure the values of other things;

(3) be durable, for if it continually wasted away its value would diminish every day and every minute;

(4) be indefinitely divisible, for otherwise it could not represent small values, and change could not be made;

(5) be capable of receiving and retaining delicate marks, in order that the different pieces of money should be readily recognized, even after they have been used for a long time;

(6) be easily distinguished even from similar substances, for otherwise counterfeits will be put in circulation by bad men; and

(7) be recognized as money by the civilized world, because it has to be used to make exchanges between citizens of different nations as well as between those of the same nation.

Gold and silver fulfill, better than any other known substance, these seven requisites for money:

(1) They have large value in small space and weight. No other substance, which exists in sufficient quantity to be used as money, contains as much value as gold does in equal space and weight.

(2) They are steady in value. Since history began, there has been only one considerable change in their value. This was after the discovery of the South American and the Mexican mines. Even then, the change was

not at all sudden. It took a great number of years to accomplish it. All other commodities have undergone repeated and sudden changes in value. It costs just about as much now to extract an ounce of gold or silver from the earth, purify it and coin it as it has cost for very many years. Since the cost of production is steady, the value (Prop. XXVIII) must be steady.

(3) They are very durable. Coins buried for ages have been dug up in Egypt which retain their former color and designs almost perfectly.

(4) They are indefinitely divisible. They lose nothing, too, by being divided. An ounce of gold is worth just as much, no matter into how many pieces it is divided. If a large diamond were quartered, it would lose 99 per cent. of its value.

(5) They can be easily coined, and they retain the forms and designs given them for a very great number of years.

(6) They cannot be easily imitated. Counterfeits of them, though made with cunning care, can be readily detected. The "ring" of gold and silver cannot be produced by any baser metal.

(7) They are the only substances recognized as money by the whole civilized world.

Therefore, gold and silver make the best money.

PROPOSITION XXXV.

Paper money, not convertible into specie at par, is an evil.

The measure of length must have length; the measure of weight must have weight; the measure of values must have value. Paper money has only a sham value, unless it is convertible into specie at par. If you can get a gold dollar by presenting a paper dollar at the bank which issues it, then paper is as good as gold, because everything is worth what it will exchange for. Paper is more convenient to carry than gold. This is the reason it is used by communities whose paper-money is convertible into specie.

Inconvertible paper money has a sham value, because the value at which it exchanges does not depend upon its cost of production. It costs only about one mill to produce a paper dollar. The reason it exchanges for more than one mill is because the bank or government issuing it promises to redeem it in specie some time. The chance of its being worth par in gold some time makes it worth something in gold now. But since its value depends upon this chance, it must change with the chance. The chance changes from day to day, and so the value of paper money changes.

This changing value makes it unfit to measure values, just as a stick which was 30 inches long to-day and 25 to-morrow and 27 the day after, would be unfit to measure length.

If it cannot measure values accurately, it cannot be a good medium of exchange. Suppose the tailor is willing to sell a coat for $20 in gold, he will not take $20 in inconvertible paper for it, because the value of such money changes from day to day, and so the $20 bill may not be worth as much as a $20 gold piece to-morrow. If $1 in paper is worth that day 50 cents in gold, he will charge about $45 for the coat. The $40 will equal the $20 gold piece, and the extra $5 will be a protection against his losing very much if the paper loses any more value. If a paper dollar is worth, the day after he sells the coat, only 40 cents in gold, then his $45 is worth only (45×40 cents=) $18, and he has then exchanged the coat for $2 less than its value, despite his extra charge of $5. If he had not made this extra charge, what he got in exchange for the coat would be worth only (40×40 cents=) $16. Then his loss would be $4.

When the money used by a nation changes value in this way, all dealers make this extra charge to protect themselves against loss in case the paper loses any more value. They sell their wares for as much paper money as will buy, that day, the gold which the wares are worth, *plus* something more as an insurance against loss by the depreciation of the paper. The wholesale dealer charges this increased price to the retailer; the retailer charges it, *plus* his own increased price, to the consumer. The consumer therefore finally pays all these extra charges, all of which he would escape, if the currency used were gold or silver, or paper convertible into specie at par. Poor people usually buy their goods of the last of a long line of wholesale and retail dealers. Each one of the line has charged this extra price. The poor therefore suffer most, in this as in other ways, from the use of inconvertible paper money.

Such money has a large (sham) value in small space and weight, but if the chance of its being some time redeemed in specie ceases to exist, then its market value falls to the level of its intrinsic value (see explanation of Prop. XXVIII), and every note, whether for one or one thousand dollars, is worth about one mill. Inconvertible paper money is very unsteady in value. The greenback dollar has varied in value all the way from $1 to 35 cents in gold. Such money is not very durable. It can, to be sure, be divided indefinitely. The stamps on it soon wear away. It can be counterfeited with comparative ease. It circulates as money only within the country of the government issuing it. When a bank issues it, it circulates only near that bank. It forms no part of the world's money.

Therefore, paper money, not convertible into specie at par is an evil.

PROPOSITION XXXVI.

The worse currency drives out the better.

When there are two legal sorts of currency in a country, the worse will drive out the better. Gold and greenbacks are both legal mediums of exchange in this country now (1875), but the greenbacks, which are the worse currency, have driven out the gold.

Suppose a shoe-manufacturer borrowed $100 in gold when we had a gold currency, and must repay the loan now (1875), when a gold dollar is worth $1.12 in greenbacks. His shoes will sell for $2 a pair in gold, and about $2.50 a pair in greenbacks. If he pays the debt in gold he will have to part with fifty pairs of shoes. If he pays it in greenbacks he will have to part with only 40 pairs. It will therefore be cheaper for him to use greenbacks. The creditor will lose by it though, because he lent $100 in gold and he gets back $100 in greenbacks, which are worth only about $89 in gold. It is one bad result of a double currency that debtor can thus defraud his creditor.

When a debtor has to pay his debt, and can pay it in a bad and cheap or a good and costly currency, he will use the cheap currency. Every debtor will do this. There will therefore be no demand for the good currency, and it will disappear from the market.

Therefore, the worse currency drives out the better.

PROPOSITION XXXVII.

Credit is not capital.

Capital (Def. 4) is wealth saved and used in production. Credit has not been saved. When a bank or a government issues a note of $100, no capital has been created. The note, if convertible into specie, represents specie and is as good as specie, but issuing it has not created the specie it represents. That existed already. Issuing the note has merely changed the owner of the specie. A has $100 in gold. He gives B in exchange for food, clothing, etc., his promise to pay $100. The total capital of the two is still only $100, plus the food and clothing unconsumed, but now B owns the $100 instead of A. B can claim it from A at any time. There has therefore been no creation of capital by creating credit.

Credit is not in itself capital. It is a lease of capital which enables a man to get the use of capital for a time, just as a lease written on a piece of parchment, which is not land, enables its holder to occupy and use land, for the time.

The creation of credit transfers the use of capital. A has $100. He lends it to B, taking in return B's written promise to pay him (A) $100, with interest, at some future time. Thus A's giving B credit has transferred the use of A's money to B. It has not created any more money or wealth. But if credit were capital, the world's wealth would now be increased by $100, since all capital is wealth.

If there were no credit, there could be no lenders, and therefore no borrowers. Only those who could use capital for their own purposes would accumulate it at all. Credit, by transferring the use of wealth from those who would not use the wealth productively to those who will, makes the wealth capital. But it is not itself capital, because it is not wealth that has been saved.

Therefore, credit is not capital.

PROPOSITION XXXVIII.

A commercial crisis is caused by the destruction, that is, the unproductive consumption, of wealth.

There are times when credit ceases; when prices suddenly fall; when merchants fail; when manufactures slacken; when wages decline and great numbers of laborers are thrown out of employment; and when bankers cease to loan money, and are unable to pay back the deposits which have been made at their banks. When this state of things exists, there is said to be a commercial crisis.

Let us see what causes all this. It is at the banks that a crisis first shows itself. We will best understand what a crisis is, therefore, by beginning to study it at the banks.

Banks gather up the savings which are made by one class of the community and loan them to another class to be employed in the production of wealth. Every $1,000 loaned by the savings banks is said to give employment, on an average, to one laborer. Let us suppose that one thousand persons each deposit $1,000 in a bank for safe-keeping. If it is left on deposit long enough, the bank will pay the owner 4 or 5 per cent. interest on it. but the bank must make more than 4 or 5 per cent., by loaning the deposit. If it did not, it would lose money. It therefore loans its deposits at 8 or 10 or 12 per cent. to persons employed in the production of wealth. Its profit consists in the difference between the interest it pays and the interest it gets.

Let us suppose that the $1,000,000 deposited by the thousand persons is loaned out to build a railroad. Then this amount of capital takes the form of a railroad. If the railroad was wanted, the company that built it will be repaid by the receipts from freights, fares, etc. The company can therefore repay the banker, and the banker his depositors. But if the railroad has been built where it was not needed, so that no use, or very little use, is made of it after it is built, then the company will receive nothing or almost nothing from freights, fares, etc. It will therefore be unable to pay the banker, and the banker therefore cannot pay his depositors.

What is the consequence of this?

The depositors run to the bank. The bank cannot pay them. It closes. The railroad company can get no more loans. It has to stop work. The labor employed in taking care of the part of the road already built, and in building the other part is thrown out of work. There is now less demand for rails, locomotives, cars, etc. The manufacturers of these things dismiss some of their hands and slacken work. But if less railroad iron is wanted, fewer men will be wanted to work the iron mines and to carry the ore from the mines to the places where it is made into rails, locomotives, car-wheels, etc. This has all happened because a railroad was produced which was not needed, that is, because $1,000,000 of deposits was consumed unproductively, or destroyed; for unproductive consumption and destruction are the same.

The unproductive consumption of the $1,000,000 has had several bad effects :

(1) It caused the bank to close;

(2) It made the depositors lose their money;

(3) It threw railroad employees out of work;

(4) It stopped the iron works where railroad iron was being manufactured;

(5) It diminished the demand for iron at the mines;

(6) It threw out of employment a number of miners, ore-carriers and iron-workers;

(7) It slackened all kinds of business, for the laborers thrown out of employment could not buy of the grocer, dry goods merchant, shoemaker, etc., as before;

(8) Consequently, the retail grocer, shoemaker, etc., were unable to buy of the wholesale dealers in groceries, boots and shoes, etc.

(9) Therefore, the wholesale dealers stopped buying, and the demand for all these articles was less, and consequently the production of them diminished.

All these evils, then, felt throughout the whole commercial body, have resulted from the destruction of the $1,000,000 worth of capital. The dollars themselves have not been consumed, but the food and clothing of the laborers they hired, and the wood, rails, bridges, rolling-stock, etc., which they bought have all been spent without producing wealth. Thus, although the dollars themselves are still in existence, $1,000,000 worth of capital has been destroyed.

Now we have only to suppose that a great many millions have been consumed unproductively in a great many other ways in order to account for all these effects on a greater scale. But when these things happen on a great scale, we have a commercial crisis.

Therefore, a commercial crisis is caused by the destruction, that is, the unproductive consumption, of wealth.

PROPOSITION XXXIX.

The effects of a commercial crisis can be removed only by the production of wealth.

The destruction of wealth (Prop. XXXVIII) causes a crisis; the production of wealth, therefore, by removing the cause, must remove the effect,— that is, the crisis.

As wealth is produced, it is deposited in banks for investment, or it is used in production without being first put in the banks. Then the laborers thrown out of work by the crisis are employed again. They are therefore able to buy again of the grocer, baker, shoemaker, etc. The latter buy fresh stocks of goods from the wholesale dealers. The wholesalers in turn give orders to the producers.

Thus business revives and times are said to be good. Wealth is produced and the effects of the crisis disappear.

Therefore, the effects of a commercial crisis can be removed only by the production of wealth.

DEFINITION 14. *A tax is a sum of money collected by a government from persons or property within its dominions.*

DEFINITION 15. *Duties are taxes on imported goods, that is, on goods brought from other countries.*

DEFINITION 16. *A tariff is a law fixing duties.*

There are two kinds of tariffs,—revenue and protective.

A revenue tariff is one the only object of which is to raise money for the needs of the government. A country which has a revenue tariff is said to enjoy "free trade." Its government does not interfere with its trade with foreign countries except for the sake of raising needed revenue.

A protective tariff is one which fixes duties in such a way that the home manufacturer can afford to produce and sell a commodity more cheaply than it can be sold after it has been imported, and the duty on it has been paid. The home manufacturer is then said to be " protected " against the competition of his foreign rivals.

A revenue tariff is for the benefit of the government. A protective tariff, while it yields some revenue to the government, is mainly for the benefit of the manufacturers.

PROPOSITION XL.

A tariff should be for revenue alone.

A protective tariff is an injustice and a hardship. An illustration will suffice to show what is meant by this. Suppose a man wants to buy cloth with which to make a coat. England manufactures some of the best cloth in the world. He says he will buy English cloth. It is better and cheaper. Now if trade were free, he might buy the cloth, we will say, for $1 a yard when imported here. American cloth of perhaps not as good quality is selling for $1.50 a yard. To keep him from purchasing the English cloth, and to compel him to buy the American, the government adds to the price of the English cloth, say 60 cents, as an extra duty. It is now worth $1.60, which is more than the buyer can afford to pay. He therefore buys the American cloth for $1.50.

Now, who has been the gainer by this? The American manufacturer. The buyer has lost 50 cents on each yard. And as the manufacturers are few, while those who use cloth are many, the whole country is made to pay out large sums by a protective tariff for the benefit of the few. This is why a protective tariff is an injustice and a hardship.

There are other reasons why trade between different countries should be free.

When it is free, each country produces those things for which it is best adapted, that is, which it can produce cheapest and best. France can produce very good and very cheap silk. England is not adapted to the cultivation of the mulberry-trees on which the silk-worms feed, and therefore cannot well produce good silk. But it can produce very good and very cheap cutlery. It is best then that it should produce good cutlery and exchange it for good French silk. If each country had to produce its own silk and its own cutlery, the result would be that France would have some very poor but very dear cutlery, while England would have some very poor but very dear silk. Both countries would suffer, and only the few engaged in the manufacture of the poor but "protected" articles would gain.

The government has no right to tax one man to benefit another. It should treat all men alike. A man has a right to buy wherever he can buy best and cheapest; but this right he cannot have when trade is not free.

It is claimed that a protective tariff benefits a country by stimulating its manufactures, and so making it independent of other countries and by securing employment for its workpeople.

But there is no more reason why a country should buy nothing from other countries than there is why a man should buy nothing of other men.

Suppose a man had to produce and manufacture his own food, clothing, house, shoes, books, church, and everything else. He would not produce nearly as much wealth in a year (Prop. X) as if he should make one thing, shoes for instance, and sell them for money, and then sell the money for his food, clothing, house-rent, books, pew, etc. So a country, by manufacturing the things which it can manufacture best, produces more wealth than if it were to try to manufacture everything. It can then exchange its surplus wealth for the special products of other countries, just as the shoemaker exchanges his surplus shoes for the products of the tailor. farmer, etc.

A protective tariff does not increase the number of workmen employed. It does not increase the capital in a country, and it therefore cannot (Prop. V) increase the amount of labor employed. It is true that if the "protected" commodities were produced abroad and im-

5

ported, as some of them would be under a revenue tariff, they would not be produced at home, at least in such quantities as they are when "protected." At least part of the labor now employed in producing them at home would therefore be no longer employed *in that way*. It would, however, be employed in another way. For, in order to pay for the goods imported, we would have to export other goods. Therefore there would have to be a greater production of the latter. The labor hitherto employed in producing at home the goods now imported from abroad, would now be employed in producing the goods exported to pay for these imports.

A high tariff "protects" only the manufacturers. The higher profits they make must be paid, of course, by the men not engaged in manufactures,— the ministers, lawyers, teachers, doctors, journalists, grocers, farmers, bakers, laborers, etc., etc. The number of persons, employers and employees, engaged in every sort of manufacture in this country in 1870 was only 2,707,421. The number of farmers alone was 5,922,471. Thus the many are taxed by a protective tariff for the benefit of the few.

Moreover, the persons engaged in manufactures all pay higher prices for the manufactured articles they consume than they would were there no protective tariff. Thus the few who gain directly also lose indirectly.

Again, the manufacturers of the protected commodities get a higher profit than they otherwise would on what they sell in the home-market, but they are restricted to this market by a protective tariff. Such a tariff shuts them out from the markets of the world. American axe-manufacturers, for instance, used to sell their wares over the whole world. Now, they cannot compete with the English manufacturers. For a high tariff has made some of their raw materials, their machinery and their labor cost so much that they can no longer produce good axes as cheaply as the English can. They are therefore undersold in all foreign countries, and can sell nothing outside of the United States. Their higher profits in the home market are often much more than counterbalanced by their loss of the profits they could make, were there only a revenue tariff, by foreign trade.

Suppose the reader, when he next sits down to breakfast, should think how much has been added to the cost of the things in the room and on the table by the present protective tariff. The table on which the breakfast is served is taxed 40 per cent., the table-cloth 42 per cent., the dishes, plates, cups and saucers 46 per cent., the plated spoons 35 per cent., the knives and forks 60 per cent., the plated coffee-pot 46 per cent., the china tea-pot 38 per cent., the salt 60 per cent., the carpet on the dining-room floor 75 per cent., the stove 45 per cent., the wall-paper 47 per cent., the glass in the windows 60 per cent., and the chairs 34 per cent.* If there were a revenue tariff, all of these articles could have been imported and sold at prices much less than we have to pay now. The American capital and labor now employed in producing some of them would then be used in the production of the wealth sent abroad in exchange for them. Thus, as much capital and labor would be employed and we should have to pay less for many necessaries.

A protective tariff tends to keep foreign articles out of the market. Americans produce similar articles and sell them at rates just below the cost of the foreign product, plus the duty. Thus a protective tariff yields the government much less money than a revenue tariff would. It merely gives high profits to a few, and makes the many pay much more for the necessaries of life than they otherwise would.

Therefore, a tariff should be for revenue alone.

* These figures are taken from the tariff of 1875.

A Summer in Norway.

With Notes on the Industries, Habits, Customs and Peculiarities of
the People, the History and Institutions of the Country,
its Climate, Topography and Productions ; also an
account of the Red-deer, Reindeer and Elk.

BY JOHN DEAN CATON, LL.D.
Ex-Chief Justice of Illinois.

8vo. 401 PAGES. ILLUSTRATED. PRICE, $2.50.

The Tribune says:

" Judge Caton is a veteran traveler. He is a man of acute observation, and
from long experience as well as natural capacity, is apt to learn something more,
and to understand and find out more, than the ordinary traveler. * * Of all
this he has made a readable and entertaining book — a book which is apt to
create in the reader a strong desire to make the same journey in person."

The Times says:

" The author of '*A Summer in Norway*' has accomplished what but few
able professional writers are capable of under the circumstances. He has given
to the public a volume of travels which will hold its own with any of like kind.
The style in which it is written is concise, terse and cheerful. The information
is solid and interesting, and a vein of genial humor pervades every page.
Throughout it is generously sprinkled with harmless, amusing incidents, deli-
cately told."

The Inter-Ocean says:

" Judge Caton has given us a work possessing all the best qualities of a
perfect book on Summer Travel. It contains neither too much nor too little ;
it is written in an easy, confidential style, without strain or affectation. As the
writer sails along by coasts and lakes and rivers, and lingers in quaint Norwegian towns, he gives us here and there just sufficient scraps of history to awaken
interest in this ancient and warlike but now peaceful and industrious people.
He has the strong, bold touch of masculine force and observation, united to a
graceful narrative style. The book from beginning to end reads like a story
told by the Judge at the head of his own table. Carlyle sits in his den at Chel-
sea, poring over 'Sagas' and ancient manuscripts ; our stalwart traveler,
accompanied by his ladies, mingles with the people, makes friends with the
' Lapps,' watches salmon fishing in the pools, sleeps in Norwegian beds, and
indulges in a little wholesome rhetoric over their narrowness and discomfort.
His book is as fresh as the mountain breezes, while his observations are full of
that kindly and appreciative feeling which can only come from a liberal mind
and a generous heart."

Mailed, post-paid, on receipt of price by the publishers.

JANSEN, McCLURG & CO.,
CHICAGO.

A New and Cheap Edition of

MEMORIES:

A STORY OF GERMAN LOVE.

TRANSLATED FROM THE GERMAN
By GEO. P. UPTON.

16mo.   Red edges; flexible covers; with new designs.   PRICE, $1.00.

The great favor with which our Holiday Edition of this remarkable book was received, and the very large sale of the same, has induced us to issue an entirely new and beautiful edition at the low and popular price above named, with the hope that it may reach the hands of every lover of pure and meritorious literature.

From the New York Tribune:

" The touching story of 'German Love,' whose tender pathos lacks only the harmonies of verse to make it one of the most exquisite poems in the German language, is here reproduced in an English costume of chaste and delicate beauty."

From the Advance, Chicago:

" This is, in every respect, an exquisitely beautiful and charming book. * * The perfection of elegance and simplicity. The story itself is one of the purest, sweetest and most fascinating that we have read for months. * * A prose poem rather than a novel."

From the Home Journal:

" The work is an admirable illustration of the richness, tenderness and depth of German sentiment, an endowment in which that people is distinguished from all others. Seldom has the dawn, the rise and the setting of the sun of passion been depicted with such sympathetic insight and such sweetness and refinement of color."

From the Chicago Tribune:

" This is one of the most charming little books we have ever read. We know of only one other story to which we can compare it — the exquisite tale of Paul and Virginia, by Bernardin de Saint-Pierre. It were difficult indeed to say which of these two little books is the more admirable. They are both gems of love stories, and those who are acquainted with the French one can have no higher assurance of the excellence of the German than that it is not its inferior in interest or poetic elevation."

" Memories " is also issued in Small Quarto, tinted paper, red border, gilt edge ; making it a beautiful gift.   Price, $2.00.

Sent by mail, post-paid, on receipt of price, by the publishers.

JANSEN, McCLURG & CO.,

CHICAGO.

TRUTHS FOR TO-DAY.

BY PROF. DAVID SWING.

A beautiful volume, containing a choice selection of the finest discourses of this eloquent preacher. 12mo, tinted paper, 325 pages. Price $1.50.

From the New York Tribune:

"The preacher makes no display of his rich resources, but you are convinced that you are listening to a man of earnest thought, of rare culture, and of genuine humanity. His forte is evidently not that of doctrinal discussion. He deals in no nice distinctions of creed. He has no taste for hair-splitting subtleties, but presents a broad and generous view of human duty, appealing to the highest instincts and the purest motives of a lofty manhood. In his view, the ethical element holds the rightful supremacy in our nature."

From Dr. Powers *in the Alliance, Chicago:*

"As sacred compositions, they captivate by a sweetness that is as natural to them as tints to the rose or flavor to the strawberry. They are logical without a display of argumentation, and poetical without any sacrifice of directness and sincerity. While one's reason is appealed to all along, the language of the appeal comes up all blossoming and fragrant with the heart. It would be hard to find in the same compass so much real poetry and logic in vital union as in these discourses. And here is the secret of their power."

From the Independent, New York:

"So far are these sermons from being hostile to true Christianity that they constitute a most powerful defense of all that is powerful and permanent in our religion. • • The American pulpit has sent forth few volumes of sermons richer in thought, more devout in sentiment, more admirable in statement, or fairer in outward fashioning, than this volume of sermons of Mr. Swing."

From the Advance, Chicago:

"Such is the glow of his rhetoric, such the beauty of his illustrations, such the generous tone of his sentiments, that the reader is soon brought into admiring sympathy with the author."

Sent by mail, post-paid, on receipt of price by the publishers.

JANSEN, McCLURG & CO.,
CHICAGO.

www.ingramcontent.com/pod-product-compliance
Lightning Source LLC
Chambersburg PA
CBHW020241090426
42735CB00010B/1791